UNITED WE LOVE

UNITED WE LOVE

*Strategies for a
Thriving Marriage*

FELIX NORTHWOOD

QuillQuest Publishers

CONTENTS

1	Introduction	1
2	Understanding the Foundation of a Strong Marriage	3
3	Effective Communication Techniques	5
4	Nurturing Emotional Intimacy	7
5	Building Trust and Honesty	9
6	Managing Conflict and Resolving Differences	11
7	Developing Shared Goals and Values	13
8	Cultivating Mutual Respect and Appreciation	15
9	Sustaining Romance and Passion	17
10	Balancing Individuality and Togetherness	19
11	Supporting Each Other's Growth and Development	21
12	Strengthening the Bonds of Friendship	23
13	Creating a Healthy Work-Life Balance	25
14	Overcoming Challenges and Adversities Together	27
15	Seeking Professional Help and Guidance	29
16	Conclusion	31

Copyright © 2024 by Felix Northwood

All rights reserved. No part of this book may be reproduced in any manner whatsoever without written permission except in the case of brief quotations embodied in critical articles and reviews.

First Printing, 2024

CHAPTER 1

Introduction

The proposed study, predominantly a review of researches on marriage, seeks to explore a few tentative strategies that could lay the foundation for a successful life-long marriage. Since there is no formula for happiness in marriage, but is context specific, strategies are the master principal or directive in this study, rather than advice. These strategies are formulated from th22e twin underlying premises that (a) the other is a person like yourself, and (b) that two people united in marriage (and procreation) make an entity in which the parts are interdependent (in relational space), and are the best (or most naturally equipped) entity to foster each other's interests. Given these landmark premises, it becomes practical to espouse practices that would appropriately emphasize the interconnectedness of the two individuals in the marriage.

There are as many books on marriage as people who preach on the topic. And yet, the prevalence of divorce in the United States, despite many courtships and fairy-tale weddings, crank out startling statistics such as, "At nearly 53%, the divorce rate is rising". How did we go from the idealized marriage to the fleeting "'til death do us part" of second-rate couples? As two people, brought together in holy matrimony, what turned buddies into foes? How do two-in-one—so in love and harmonious—end up divided, wrangling over freedom for one and equity for the other that ends in irreversible emotional divergences? Since it takes two to tango, why do they then dissolve the marriage?

CHAPTER 2

Understanding the Foundation of a Strong Marriage

Marriage is a living principle. It breathes and expands and flourishes in relationship.

The above quote from Pres. Gordon B. Hinckley has been an inspiration and a guide in my marriage. Both my husband and I have worked to strengthen and enrich our relationship with the Savior, our marriage, and our family. This statement of the prophet has been my motto in times of trials, in good days and in bad days, when we celebrated our anniversary married or separated. It is not enough to establish a good marriage; the relationship with our Heavenly Father needs to be established as if we were uniquely treated by Him.

We need to have the spirit of the Lord constantly, just like we need air to breathe. It is important to remember for those engaged in the process of dating and marriage that relationships are based on feeling, emotion, beauty, and fragile material. They are the spiritual counterpart needed to be safe in the care of the Savior. Establishing marriage with the support of the Atonement and the Savior's doings is a way to avoid despair and emotional collapse in feelings. Remember that marriage is not only made up of two people who come to live together in partnership - yoga style - marriage is made up of three people: husband, wife, and Savior. As we establish our marriage to Christ, we find more satisfaction and real and permanent joy.

CHAPTER 3

Effective Communication Techniques

In any type of communication, one must bear in mind that words represent only a fraction of the communication process. In the case of a couple, it is body language, emotions, and feeling states. What type of emotion is attached to that tone of voice? Is intelligence, sex, or will at work? Intelligence can sometimes block emotional expression by only providing questions and answers that relate to the head, not the heart. Such as when conflict arises, perhaps quick thought criticism ensues, with a list of could haves, should haves, would haves based on personal judgment, but never really ceasing long enough to intersect with unified heart within reasonable.

The process of becoming aware of and expressing one's true emotions, desires, fears, and confrontational issues is known as awareness and self-disclosure. One of the communication techniques is grounding, in this case, self-disclosure by using self-awareness. One will immediately feel how grounded they become by opening up and sharing their true unconditional love with their spouse. Your foundation and trust in each other will become rock solid, and you both are freed up to journey through your individual selves together, exploring and appreciating each other's interests and feelings with love, rather than feeling as though you are walking through an armed minefield. As you begin to accept your spouse's feelings and not immediately trying to funnel them into a solution or try to fix them when they're not needed.

CHAPTER 4

Nurturing Emotional Intimacy

One meaningful way of maintaining and improving emotional intimacy is to deepen self-awareness, and in so doing, deepen understanding and appreciation of things that matter to loved ones. The journey toward greater self-awareness involves more than just self-reflection to learn about oneself, but also the capacity to consider others and act thoughtfully and in supportive ways. Prior research has suggested that through the course of marriage, emotional intimacy and deeper self-awareness develop over a longer course of the relationship. Emotionally healthy and satisfying marriages involve self-disclosures that further the understanding of spouses and foster depth of intimacy. Encouraging intimacy building, like working with couples in emotionally focused therapy (EFT), can shift distressful marital demands for protection and separation, or attacks for criticisms, into expressions of unfulfilled need that foster interactions rooted in emotional growth, security, and continued connection. Conveying understanding about a spouse's greater emotions in a manner emphasizing caring and compassion while avoiding criticism, clarification is an appropriate response to a partner's self-disclosure. For instance, if a spouse appreciates a sunrise, responding with "I understand how much you value experiencing together the beauty of creation" is more effective than "I don't think you really understood what I told you: I shared that we should come back here together." The willingness to engage procedures in an emotionally involved manner can enhance emotional generativity reported throughout the cycles of marriages, aligning pair members to engage in fewer conflicts with better yielded results. Better yet, these practices might lead from marrying someone who is love and the spirit of marriage to serving and walking with the rich toward a hopeful and fulfilling journey.

Emotional intimacy is not only about talking, but also about connecting. It's about seeing and being seen, supporting, encouraging, reassuring, and urging one another. In "United We Love: Strategies for a Thriving Marriage," we define emotional intimacy as "the ability to interact in an empathetic and caring manner, intentionally choosing words that will encourage a more positive interaction, which enhances our loving connection." It's self-disclosure and self-discovery, sharing the emotions of everyday life.

CHAPTER 5

Building Trust and Honesty

Exercise trust when making decisions about your future. When you honor the commitment the two of you made to each other, trust grows. Talk with each other about your private thoughts, your personal meanings, and your emotional feelings. Show signs of trust, in other words, show love, compassion, and nonverbal support. Life in your personal world and with your significant other will see through challenges. Trust and honesty will help you overcome those challenges. As you create new relationship patterns, uncontrolled emotions attached to memories of the past are likely to surface. Memories have a way of pushing your emotional hot buttons and become fuel for arguments. Practice these strategies: Cognitive self-regulation to disengage from conflicts, and recast your partner's position in the heat of the moment to understand why their reaction seems inappropriate.

When you need help with your personal life, what do you do? You go to the one person you trust to make things better. Let that place be your partner's touch, smell, kiss, laugh, and emotional warmth. Keep in mind the following strategies to build trust and honesty when you're faced with everyday problems. Trust and honesty strengthen emotional and physical intimacy. When you feel you can honestly share with your partner, you're more likely to be emotionally and physically connected. When your connection is physical, you may be motivated to maintain good health and feel more successful, whether at work, on the playing field, or socially. All of that translates to a better marriage.

CHAPTER 6

Managing Conflict and Resolving Differences

To minimize conflict, practice good listening skills, keep an open mind, and respect each other's point of view. Understand that you can only control your behavior, and it's your reaction to disputes that shape your marriage long-term. If your spouse is unhappy, it's your responsibility to take constructive control about turning challenges into opportunities. Notice and respect your partner's efforts. Acknowledge their contribution frequently – this subtle show of appreciation can make a world of difference. Express honest gratitude and never take accomplishments for granted.

Resolve disagreements through negotiation in an attempt to find an agreeable middle ground. Most issues aren't deal-breakers. A fair compromise takes trust by both individuals involved. When questions of right or wrong arise, accept fault when you approach an impasse, while understanding you're both contributing in some egocentric way. Work to identify those ways and fight against such self-seeking behavior.

Conflict arises in marriage for multiple reasons - poor communication skills being the primary cause. When navigating the waters of a conflict, it's critical to stop the blame game, be patient, and work toward resolving your differences. Quick tip: save your marriage by refusing to counter-attack. If both sides are building resentment, it's advisable to call a timeout and revisit the issue when emotions are better managed. Remember: for the marriage to survive, it's the team that wins. By adopting a "fair-fighting rule," you're making the conscious decision to put your relationship above individual arguments, and this type of sacrificial decision is a definite sign of maturity.

CHAPTER 7

Developing Shared Goals and Values

The first step in making decisions about these shared issues is to spend time communicating with your mate. Share your thoughts about things that matter to you with your mate and ask her to do the same. This is one of the keys to developing a deep and meaningful relationship. When you are able to get past the feeling that you must defend your case in an argument, communicate in a form that makes your mate feel loved, or give up because the jokes are sad, you will realize that life itself and your relationship with your partner improve greatly. While discussing vital issues together, during moments of disagreement, it is important to remind yourself that rather than feeling attacked, your mate is trying to show you how the world looks through their eyes - therefore allowing you to have a broader perspective.

When couples have a strong sense of their shared priorities, aim together at fulfilling those priorities, combine their strengths to overcome challenges and move in the same direction, the relationship that unifies them flourishes and helps them to grow together.

For a relationship to thrive, both partners need to work together - striving to fix problems whenever they arise. This is how the narrative of transformation occurs in all relationships. Without shared goals, knowledge, strategies, and proactive attitudes, it would be very difficult for a couple to move forward together and cultivate a vision of a more united relationship.

CHAPTER 8

Cultivating Mutual Respect and Appreciation

Some of the greatest sources of smiles at our Unity Picnics are the stories and speeches shared by our dear couple friends and family members, who speak of their marital experiences and end with wonderful examples that affirm mutual respect and appreciation. Smiles always in tow, those insightful and powerful examples reminded Luis and me to never take each other for granted and shifted our focus onto the breadth of kind and loving words and gestures we share with each other. From the seemingly mundane to the grandiose, the gestures of love shared between two people who are deeply in love should demonstrate how fortunate they feel to have one another.

Cultivating mutual respect and appreciation is your responsibility to create an environment of respect for each other in your marriage. It is also up to you to make a conscious effort to value each other and the relationship you have. Communicate this respect and value to your mate. Without a doubt, the mutual respect I have for Luis and the many ways I show him that respect have not only modeled what I want from him but also what he should expect from me. By daily showing each other how important and valuable you are to each other, you open yourself up to less hurt, reduced tension, and perceive and appreciate each other in the most loving ways. In other words, you and your partner are positioned to reveal the best of yourselves to each other.

CHAPTER 9

Sustaining Romance and Passion

Danish philosopher Søren Kierkegaard, who did not marry himself, recognized and even extolled the value in marriage as being an important, if not the most important, responsibility of humankind. Writing vigorously about the challenges of life, faith, and relationships, he insisted that the mutual shaping of lives through vows of marriage is more profound than the fleeting promises found in anyone else. It is through the anticipation and the sustaining force of that mutual shaping that a marriage can persist, thrive, and become a fire that vanquishes the comfortable silence of lingering life itself. Sociologist Judith Wallerstein is another intellectual who tackled the question of a romantic marriage. Based on interviews conducted over the course of more than 30 years, she concluded that all married individuals experience moments of insecurity, fear, betrayal, and irritability - and still maintain interest in their partners. Whether she was delving into the life of a woman sitting in a corner apartment room, surrounded by willow-pattern china, or a wealthy, important man captivated by the fashion and furies of post-war

America, Wallerstein recognized that a universal key to the vibrancy, happiness, and vitality in marriage involved finding those mutual joys and interests that sustained passion and "maintained the pulse and excitement of a romantic life."

One of the greatest challenges to a happy, enduring, and romantic marriage is the one that demystifies romance: romance in marital intimacy tends to decrease over time. Innumerable books, movies, music, and media entertain society's romance with romance. The work of romance is the story of overcoming - intrigue, conflict, drama, and excitement. Yet while these stories can last for many seasons on a television screen, the story of real life can seem to be inclined toward tranquility rather than risk, simplicity rather than fire. Maintaining endearing romance over the years always requires effort. It requires more than just going through the motions of romantic love.

CHAPTER 10

Balancing Individuality and Togetherness

An example of personal space in marriage is, to some, the space needed to quiet their minds to commune with their Maker in solitary moments of prayer, meditation, or other forms of worship. To some others, it means an opportunity to relax, engage in intellectual discourse, monitor their dreams, and set spiritual, social, personal, financial, or career development goals. Balancing quality time with solitude is a winning formula for any marriage, not just those looking for a spiritual boost. This is so, for cementing a marriage and developing a deeper sense of self requires dedication, perseverance, a strong will, and time to reconnect with one's core personal essence before the marriage molded the soul into a collective identity. Two people in love do not shrink or lose their individuality in the union. Two people in love are people of their time. They are individuals in their collective being. Once they step across the threshold of the altar, the consciousness they absorbed earlier should be a witness to the world that their individualism is not lost in their sense of unity.

Each takes something from the past to contribute to a better future. Both reap benefits from the individuality of their partner.

    Peer down the memory lane of your marriage, or that of well-loved couples around you, or even the characters in romantic classics to see the value of balancing individuality with togetherness for a magical marriage. It is noble and practical advice. What has bamboozled us in marriage and other relationships is the wisdom to believe it true and more so, how to balance them. We need both individuality and togetherness to be happy. The former provides identity and separation, and the latter connectedness and unity. Put them together and the odds of a successful relationship are greatly enhanced. In marriage, two people come together with their unique backgrounds, heritages, experiences, socialization, and families. To build a strong bond and explore the full potential of the marriage, individually and collectively, they will find the need to embrace elements of their individuality even in the togetherness of the marriage. This will be beneficial to their lives as individuals and as a couple.

CHAPTER 11

Supporting Each Other's Growth and Development

By trusting in that connection to support one another, we are opening ourselves up to performing individual tasks. According to Dan Sullivan's model, it is essential for us to do this for the betterment of ourselves so that ultimately, everyone in the family as well benefits. This becomes a beautiful and harmonious exchange where everyone's needs are met. Our ability to effectively fulfill multiple roles is enhanced, and we can trust that as a collaborative team – as United We – we become an unstoppable force. Both of us sharing and providing that solid connection within the relationship, the family and the other communities in which we belong allows continuous growth. It's like being part of the grandest hybrid family laboratory where everyone has their own lab bench but each experiment has unlimited access to the others, helping them with those finer details on the latest process.

When it comes to our partners, it's a natural inclination to want to provide a safe, supportive, and loving environment in which they can flourish. If you are familiar with Dan Sullivan's 4C model of success, one of the key ingredients is Connection. The need for that connection is pervasive in the workplace, and its value to our personal relationships cannot be overstated either. How do we create a "container" in which our partner can feel safe enough to open up to us knowing that no matter what they have to tell us, they can trust that they are loved unconditionally? This container can include acts that provide comfort, signs of affection such as hugs and kisses; actively opening yourself to communicate with your partner with curious questions, real listening and a willingness to set aside any judgments about your partner's decisions or choices. This is meant to envelope your partner within a space that helps them relax into a gentle scenario where they can let go of their conscious fears and concerns.

CHAPTER 12

Strengthening the Bonds of Friendship

Calvin's image of marriage and God permeates the theological and pedagogical experience of conjugal love, as these are expressed by Madame Geneviève Carlier and Rev. Jean Paul Ribot on the pages of Uniteds: A Program of Emotional and Affective Education for Couples, where they describe marriage as a journey of appointment, as a series of lived engagements, through the moments of Narcissus love, looking at each other as a guide, and always looking together at the "magic mirror" that brings them back to God's dream of love visa with them: the Holy Scripture that promises love.

In his Institutes of the Christian Religion, John Calvin, one of the great fathers of modern Protestant Christianity, taught that the church was to be God's faithful spouse, that it should act in all matters as a devoted, loving spouse would toward the other. Calvin also said that the church is to turn to the Word, to the Holy Scriptures, as the Church's "Magic Mirror," that is, the place in the Bible where the church could see not only its flaws and sins, but also know about God's desire to love, forgive, and renew the community and each of its members, as the parable of the Prodigal Son showed. For in the mirror of the scriptures, the Church is also able to know that God speaks to us about how much he loves us and wants us as His children and heirs of His promises.

CHAPTER 13

Creating a Healthy Work-Life Balance

It is crucial that couples communicate about taking needed time away to recharge. Helping your partner recognize their work-life imbalances, as well as pointing out when they have not yet brought their "whole self" to moments where nothing work related needs to take place will greatly improve relational satisfaction. Schedule reminder dates with something your partner enjoys to encourage work-life balance. Engage with your partner regarding their ideas of work-life balance, and do not sour them with your own perceptions. Engage in shared understandings and effort to keep home spaces and adult areas as home and adult furniture; ensure you have the environmental separations from your work so that when you are home, you are present. Better psychological well-being will result – and some sophisticated problem solving – if you allow your spouse a space to turn on his or her economy and peruse what work you ought to do, assert themselves when not managed by someone else, and share their personal rewards of achievement with a partner.

In an age where technology factors heavily into both our personal and professional lives, it is increasingly difficult to get away from the office. But research indicates that a healthy work-life balance is strongly associated with better relational stability. Consider the following: On the job stress has had a spillover effect that negatively impacts marital behaviors, including inconsistency, on the part of the employee. Having an imbalance between work and life means there is potential for stress to extend beyond the office, impacting perceptions of self-worth and self-management. Conflict with a spouse has been tied to increased absenteeism, decreased organizational citizenship behavior, and a greater likelihood for suspended discipline or termination from employment.

CHAPTER 14

Overcoming Challenges and Adversities Together

The challenge: How to stay related to yourself and your partner as you get older? The proposed solution: Create a no-problem pair of minds (spirit intelligence) in each, and united intelligence between the pair of minds. United minds have their own connections, aptly interacting with all relatives or integrated groups, following their well-accepted principles, doing everything they decided to do wisely. Principles are evolutionarily adaptive natural or scientific laws or prior experiences, to remove all problems, until each or both minds move themselves outside "inside" problems to any location in an amorous infinity. Interpersonally related to all relatives, their discoveries were how to clarify their minds to world problems and they taught their necessarily related mind-sharers to do the same.

In the past 63+ years together, Mint (a publishing executive) and I (a writer) have had our share of challenges and adversities. I came to realize that the challenge is not the problem, the real problem is: How do you get to the solution? Solutions have included extending our family, adding new people such as our closest relatives, beloved friends, trusted mentors, and even adversaries and natural or scientific laws. Solutions also included extending outside of our family and into the world. Our recommended partners for marriage are not perfect people who do perfect things but are perfectly united halves, so even when one is helping the half who is disabled or devastated in bed to tell the story, smilingly, saying to children, the storyteller shall never be disabled.

CHAPTER 15

Seeking Professional Help and Guidance

When I speak of seeking help, you should also undergo marital counseling/courses to be assisted. Marriage enhancement therapies are essential. How many books have you read on marriage to better your marriage, and yet you claim to have been married for many years? New ways to re-energize your relationship and keep it fresh shouldn't escape your attention. Remain a committed student of everything aimed at making your marriage better. The more advanced education, the more likely the success of your marriage becomes. Commit yourself to acquire new knowledge that advances your married life. Keep yourself abreast and knowledgeable about the health of your marriage high on your priority list. Your marriage will thank and reward you with great happiness, satisfaction, and fulfillment in every way.

There are times when the marriage has become worn out, necessitating professional help. This is a call for courage to the couple to walk into a marriage therapist's door and get professional guidance in solving their marital issues. Time wasters and falsehoods such as "we are happy, comfortable, or things are OK as they are" are just old adages which only pose as masks to the real issues. Seeking professional guidance could be one in a series of interventions that will help both of you speak the same language again. Marriage therapists are trained in various approaches to help and make your relationship move on.

CHAPTER 16

Conclusion

If you ask couples what their secrets are to the success of their marriages, they can articulate it directly, but not all share big insights. Love—real love—thrives in a couple's ability to honor, accept and support each other. All of these actions are gifts that feed the honest and tangible qualities of real love. Any love can thrive and keep on growing by companionate love that is built by caring for each other. That is the glue to hold solidly all the unspoken and inarticulate bonds of real love. It provides strength and preserves that love through conflicts and all the other perils of married life.

You are a strong partner, and you are capable of having a strong marriage. Developing the capacity to love, support, and tolerate each other—especially during times of hardship—is the fabric of a strong, healthy partnership. Openness, flexibility, and patience nurture that capacity, and love flows all over your world. Being able to do everything "halfway" together, while not saying or acting too often disagreeably to one another, not hating your disagreements with each other, not constantly fighting for a "better tomorrow", just works wonders for many couples.

Conclusion

Milton Keynes UK
Ingram Content Group UK Ltd.
UKHW040740301124
451843UK00010B/231